Thirteen Short Poems

◆ ◆ ◆

And a Draft of XXX Sonnets in Prose

Steve — from John — May 2023

JOHN MATTHIAS

DOS MADRES
2023

DOS MADRES PRESS INC.
P.O. Box 294, Loveland, Ohio 45140
www.dosmadres.com editor@dosmadres.com

Dos Madres is dedicated to the belief that the small press is essential to the vitality of contemporary literature as a carrier of the new voice, as well as the older, sometimes forgotten voices of the past. And in an ever more virtual world, to the creation of fine books pleasing to the eye and hand.

Dos Madres is named in honor of Vera Murphy and Libbie Hughes, the "Dos Madres" whose contributions have made this press possible.

Dos Madres Press, Inc. is an Ohio Not For Profit Corporation and a 501 (c) (3) qualified public charity. Contributions are tax deductible.

Executive Editor: Robert J. Murphy

Illustration & Book Design: Elizabeth H. Murphy
www.illusionstudios.net

Typeset in Adobe Garamond Pro & Iowan Old Style
ISBN 978-1-953252-78-4
Library of Congress Control Number: 2023935014

First Edition

Published by Dos Madres Press, Inc.

CONTENTS

Part I

Part II

A Note on the Sonnets

In 2000 I published a sequence of prose passages mixed with verse called "Pages from a Book of Years." This has more than a superficial similarity to the prose sonnets in this book, but I consider it to be a sequence of poems. The prose sonnets are prose. I had thirty sections of these in mind from the beginning because I was thinking of Ezra Pound's *A Draft of XXX Cantos* and Geoffrey Hill's prose poems in *Mercian Hymns*.

For the use made here of Hill's posthumous volume, *The Book of Baruch by the Gnostic Justin,* I thank his shade and regret that there will be no further Geoffrey Hill books to scourge and challenge us. Similar thanks are due to the authors of my other two sources, Marie Étienne's *King of a Hundred Horses* (in Marilyn Hacker's translation) and Lyn Hejinian's *Oxota: A Short Russian Novel.* It was Étienne and Hejinian who suggested by their example my own experiment of writing prose sonnets.

Finally thanks are due to the editors of *Image* magazine for printing a selection from the sonnets in their issue 14, fall 2022.

◆ Part I ◆

(Thirteen Short Poems)

The Scent of Smoke

Seeking a quote, I reach for an old
Shakespeare volume on my shelf, and
Open it on the desk. Two others
In the old Collins series, 1958 or 1959,
Fall on the floor. Picking them up
And putting them beside the volume
I had sought, I distinctly smell
The scent of smoke from a wood fire
Somewhere. It is from the books.
I take a volume in my hand and open
It wide, and rudely poke my nose
Into the crotch of the breaking spine.
That sends me spinning back in time
To early visits in a Suffolk house
In Hacheston. Memory aroused, I
Can see where these four books had
Rested on the high, wide mantle
Of the central fireplace in this house
Where one still prepared wood fires in
Individual rooms when it was cold.
The mantle was formed by a large beam
On whose terms the room's structure
Organized itself. On it rested medals,
Gold plates memorializing campaigns
In two World Wars, a small sword with
An engraved blade, and the four
Collins Shakespeares. It seemed then
A temptation to recite a monologue
From Henry IV or V. The open fire
Had scorched the leather covered books

Until they smelled so much of smoke
And fire they seemed an invitation
For a winter's truce, a Christmas Eve
Fraternization like the famous one
In World War I.
                                        Captain Adams
Sat on one side of the fire, the evening
Paper in his lap, and cleaned his pipe.
Mrs. Adams could be heard preparing
Dinner with the daily help, Miss Revel,
I sat facing the Captain. Then stood up
And chose the Collins volume that held
King Henry's speech at Agincourt. Then
As now, I was seeking a quote. It was
A passage that a Brit most likely would have
Known by heart, obliged to memorize it
In his primary school. Silently I read the speech,
Remembering Olivier in the film I'd
Seen in my own elementary school where
Movies came to replace our memories of
Things we'd been told, and stories
Well-remembered by the old.
                                                  On the carpet
Well behind the fire, but still in its glow,
My two daughters played with their mother's
Toy farm. One of them complained that there
Were too many cows and insufficient pigs.
Diana, my wife, was upstairs looking for
The pigs. But there were just enough hens
For the chicken coop, and there was one
Fine rooster to announce the dawn. As this
Was Christmas Eve, my daughter Laura

Had somewhere found a small box and made
A manger in a corner of the farm. Cynouai,
Her sister, could not decide which animal would
Make the best approximation of the Human
Child divinity who ought to lie in it. The farm had
Donkeys, but neither girl could find a camel
Or a wise man, so Farmer Jones and an old horse
Were made to serve. Eventually, a lamb
Went in the manger.
"More pigs,"
Diana said as she entered the room,
And everyone looked up. She gave the room
A sense of purpose and of art. The Captain
Smoked his pipe, I closed the Collins Shakespeare,
My daughters reached out hands for pigs, and
Mrs Adams said that dinner had been served
Next door. All of this at once!

At some point I brought back
The set of Shakespeare to our Indiana home—
The Suffolk house
Was sold, and Hacheston itself became
A village haven for London commuters.
The books have
Rested on some high shelves for
Many years, but I'd not much consulted them.
The print's too small now for my failing eyes
And I'm as old as Captain Adams was
That Christmas. There are no children in my house
And my wife died two years ago. But now
There seems to be some smoke in every room
From something not contained as fire was

In that Suffolk grate. I breathe it in like poison
Or like smoke from lotus flowers. The book
Itself seems like a fading coal in my hands.
I find the passage I was looking for, but have
No longer any need to write it down.

A Memory

Times past I was proud of my memory.
I could reconstruct both sides of a conversation
That occurred fifty years ago; I could name
The authors and titles of the first couple of dozen
Books on, say, the third tier of my bookshelf
On being challenged to do it. And I was sometimes
Set other tasks: Remembering why I was in pain
For example; remembering why I had been happy.
A friend remembers an early death among the
Group of people we knew in California, a suicide.
Shall we all say his name? "Thrice blessed,"
Said Mandelstam, "is he who puts a name in
His song." My friend does not remember the name
Of the man who died (who killed himself) and
Substitutes the generic "student." I, too, remember
Roughly the circumstances of the tragedy.
A grad student in classics left a note and drove
Out to the beach and drowned himself. All of
This fifty years ago. After reading the poem I
Start thinking of all those who have died from
My years in California. Some went to Vietnam,
Some to Canada as exiles, some kept at the grind
And ended up as professors. But this young man
Only drove as far as the ocean and swam out to the
Point when he knew he could never swim back.
I cannot think of his name. I write an email to my
Girlfriend of those years because she was a major
In classics and surely knew him as he was a
Fellow student in Greek and Latin classes. He was
A wealthy easterner, my friend's poem recalls.

My girlfriend was from Bettendorf, Iowa. She
Writes back that she has no memory of the event
Or the person whose death I describe. I fear
She thinks I'm confused, but I'm not. I remember
With great clarity her account of the death, I
Remember her tears, I remember everything
Except for the young man's name. She had been
A friend of his, I remember that with certainty.
I write to the poet whose poem set all of this in
Motion by publishing his poem. What, I ask, was
Our fellow student's real name? He writes back
That he doesn't remember, and that's why
The name's not in his poem, but only an
Account of the death of a "student of classics."
Two years ago, a year ago, I could have
Supplied the name. At least I remember my
Girlfriend's tears, the department closing down
For a day in his memory, an old professor's
Aching grief as he spread the word. What was
The name? The name has become Anon.
A non-named in hey nonny no a noman poem.
Blessed is he who puts a name in his song.

A Late Style

She, your mother, was only just fourteen
When she fell in love with your grandfather's ward,
The natural son of his dead brother who spent
His summers in a Tennessee mountain shack and
His winters reading Kant and Schopenhauer
To educate himself for the menial tasks he performed
In the D.C. office of your mother's dad, who was
The U.S. Senator from Tennessee. The ward's name was
Aubrey Tucker Bradshaw, and in that year when
Trudy was fourteen, he was twenty-one.

When I say *your mother*, *your grandfather*,
Your this or that, I'm often thinking of the narrator
In the last book you managed to write, working
With an amanuensis and slowly dictating
Between strokes and with other infirmities a prose
One critic called "so graceful and lucid one has
The impression that it simply happened,
Dropping from the heavens onto the page"—
And when I say *you*, I also mean "you the author,"
And willingly conflate the maker of the book
With a character, something we've all been
Taught not to do since school days and for the
Best of reasons—
                                        Your mother, then,
The Senator's daughter and
Kin to her early flame, Aubrey Tucker Bradshaw—
Bradshaw the name of Aubrey's mother
Whose lover died and left the first family of the state
An illegitimate son, cousin to the Senator's

Three daughters and enigma to his
Grandson—you—insofar as all of this is told
By the narrator whose memory we cling to in
Our confusion, saying you, you—

It all starts on a train. The senator has died
And his body, resting in an elaborate coffin, is guarded
In turn by his three sons-in-law and sometimes
By Aubrey, whom all the others disdain and who
In their turn are disdained by him, the ward. The train
Includes a baggage car for the coffin and
Two pullmans for the Senator's three daughters,
Their husbands, and the child-version
Of the grown-up narrator who's inspired
In large part by the dead man's famous "stories"
Which have been re-told, with variations, down
The years—but not, of course, told on the journey
Bearing "the most popular man in the Senate" and a friend
Of William Howard Taft, president at the time—1916—
And himself an eager audience for the dead man's tales.
The train's sorrowful ride is from Washington to Nashville
And people line the tracks, just as they had for Lincoln.
In Nashville he lay in state, and then resumed his
Journey to Knoxville station, during which, or maybe
Shortly after the arrival, Aubrey Tucker Bradshaw
Simply disappears—
                                        "Train of thought," we say,
"Flowing River of Words." From Aubrey's disappearance
You could tell your tale at leisure, follow parenthetical
Associations out of bounds to non-sequiturs if it
Should please, wait with patience while your mother
Said her poems—"Trudy tell us 'Laska,' 'Snowbound,'

'Locksley Hall'"—but don't place a jar in Tennessee
The way some modern poet might, breaking it
To signify the lost state of Franklin, ghosting still
In isolation after war with North Carolina, place in which
To disappear that might, like Brigadoon, only come
Alive again on one day of the year.

Hiding in that figurative Franklin of his mind,
Aubrey was sometimes glimpsed or heard about—
A name spoken in a restaurant coming from
A conversation's reference to a Colonel Bradshaw-Tucker;
A colleague's recounting of a story he had heard from
A man called A.N. Bradshaw, "an urbane and
Distinguished-looking person with a Van Dyke beard
And wearing a kind of Prince Albert coat with tails";
A presence in the house of a Rhode Island socialite
Who passed through a door with his double on her arm;
Even in a bit of newspaper—*The Washington Post*—
Used to wrap up lettuce from a visit to the marketplace
Which revealed, when unwrapped and laid down flat
An ageing but familiar face. It was like discovering
A Sappho fragment on the unwound winding cloth
Of a mummy—

In the course of this you passed your final years,
You the author, while the *you* who is
A character traces his own life from would-be artist
To a narrow art historian working on the Pre-Raphaelites.
Through it all, Aubrey's still spotted at the edge of things
From time to time.
                                        It's mostly at funerals when
He appears, lurking at the back of the funeral home,

The church, the graveside family group, as one by one
The daughters and the sons-in-law of the Patriarch
Begin to die. And so time passes, and you—both character
And author—age into your final postures, crouched
Over a desk with pen in hand, one writing on Pre-Raphaelites,
The other on the family for which the first both champions
And laments archaic habits and old traditions in which
A man could find himself a ward—

And you, my own
First teacher of the reach of an imagination and
The possibility of breaching conventions which the
Public life of old families, mine as well as yours, might
Wish upon their young, finally summoned Aubrey back
At the end of your book. Wearing electrodes on your
Legs to kill the neuropathic pain, leaning on a cane,
And fearing yet another stroke, you ended by
Dictating Aubrey's reappearance as transfigured man,
Freed of his wardship, but also invalid like you,
Weird of expression, hyperbolic in his speech, fierce
In his strangeness—his history of moving through
His secret life as thing self-created—

And so, like
Your hero Henry James, you're forced
To dictation at the end, spinning sentences that
Your amanuensis strains to gather on the page.
He sees that your eyes are looking not at him
But vaguely into space, and that your story's
left the realm of ink and paper and begun to
Take possession of your body. "Often," your
Amanuensis wrote, "Peter would suddenly laugh
And turn to me and look with sudden joy in
His face, delighting with the hapless teller's

Misunderstanding of his tale, struggling with
His vain attempts to untangle tangles of his
Own delusional musings."

                    You and you I praise.
The tangler and untangler both. Teller and the told.
Who, a critic said, would ever guess that such
A frail old man could write such a vital book. And who
Would think that such a book could write
In its strange written way such a youthful, vital man.

i.m. Peter Taylor and *In the Tennessee Country*

The Centuries and Yves Bennefoy

The Falklands War! It seems like something
That happened in another century. It *did*
Happen in another century. We were in Roussillon;
I had with me a travel guide to the south
Of France and an anthology of French poems.
I had a morning paper at our breakfast table
And opened it to read about Mrs. Thatcher
Proclaiming that her forces were *les plus*
Marveilleuse du monde . . . and on she went
Sounding like she thought she was Napoleon.
I tore out the article and slipped it in the book
Of poems; later in the day I managed to get
Her remark into a poem of my own that also
Quoted Yves Bonnefoy because some lines
From his work in the anthology mentioned
"Jean et Jeanne,' which sounded good together
And which I therefore took as the name
Of "one low ruined house in Perpignan."
I wrote that when "the great winds passed
The threshold of that house, nothing sang
Or appeared." Or maybe I translated it from
The Bonnefoy poem. After that, what I wrote
Trailed off and got diverted, saying something
About "the arch daughter of shadows," building
"A fire in a cold great hall" and graying faces
"Falling like the plaster of day . . ."

At the moment

When there's no war in the Falklands but
Rather a terrible war in Ukraine, something
Leads my idle hand to reach for a book

By Yves Bonnefoy on my shelf. Out of it
Falls a letter—or, rather, what we've come to
Call a "thread," an email continuum dated
July 21 2008 at the top. Such letters didn't
Come to me electronically at the time of
The Falklands War. If you were going to
Enclose a letter you'd received from someone
Else with one of your own, you'd fold it up
And put it in an envelope with a stamp affixed.
It was understood that you might not have been
Doing that with the first person's permission.
It's all much easier with email to forget
About another's privacy. In any case, it is no
Longer necessary to communicate with fires
From mountain tops the way the Roman Valarius
Was obliged to do from the tour de Madeloc
Along the backbone of the Pyrenees near where
We stayed in Roussillon. All that signaling
With fires seems something from another century.
It was something from another century.
But now I have the email printout unfolded
On my lap. From what it says, I must have finished
What I now remember as an unfinished poem
As Tony Rudolf found it in a magazine and wrote
"I happened to read your poem 'A Wind in Roussillon'
And faxed it to a friend in Port-Vendres, Augustus Young,
And also to Yves Bonnefoy, who writes me in an email:
Oui, je reconnais bein mon poeme 'Jean et Jeanne'
Et suis tout prêt à le laisser vivre in another country.
He writes "in another country" in English. I had
Evidently said in the finished poem that I'd forgotten
That "the low ruined house called Jean et Jeanne"

Was "in another country." But what did I know?
Yves Bonnefoy goes on, *Jean et Jeanne sont deux*
Menhirs isolés, mais assez proches l'un de l'autre
Sur un lande de Belle-île en mer. C'est ainsi
Qu'on les nomme, sur cette île. Having puzzled all
That out, I Google "Jean et Jeanne" on Belle-île
And there are the menhirs.
Jean was son of a bard,
And Jeanne was a shepherdess; they were forbidden
By Druids to become the lovers that they already were.
I can see the standing stones, separated by a distance
Just too far for Jean and Jeanne to stretch their arms
And touch. They broke the laws of cast and Druids
Caused a local witch to work the spell that turned them
Into stones. This I did not know. And yet there is the
Low ruined house in Roussillon as well that's named
For them. I think that may be where they went on
Certain nights when the moon was full and Druids
And the witch relented until dawn the following day.
How sad and brave they look as stones. On Belle-île
They've stood for centuries waiting for the full moons
While Valarius lit signal fires, kings sent their heralds,
Bonaparte issued commands, and eventually the
Likes of us, with wars far away for a time, posted
Air-letters, sent out documents by fax, and even
discovered our mistakes if a forgotten printed email
Happened to drop from a book in our own century.

Schiller's Totenkopf

In what charnel house did Goethe's hand
Stir among the scattered bones, see
Dead forms arise to adept's eye, arms and legs
Detached and mixed with hands and feet
Belonging to a score of dead, limbs once
Zierlich tatge Glider—"full of grace"—all among,
As an English hand might render it, "unjointed
Shoulder blades"—*entrenkte Schulterblatter.*

Alas poor Schiller, Goethe knew you well
And held your much-loved memory
In his mind while in his hands he held
Your skull. Werter's, Maister's maker
Took you for a brother when you urged
Abandonment of pet distractions—rocks
And color theory and a dozen other things—
To get you back to finishing your *Faust.*

Did Euphorion fall like Icarus the moment
Goethe plucked that skull among the many
Gathered like potatoes out of Weimar's boneyard,
1826? The cemetery's old historian would write:
However ardent the conviction, the Sexton said
Identity was most uncertain. Still, the skull was claimed
By Goethe who in *terza rima* lifted up his relic of
"A rare nobility" that still was in his care when

Faust took linden from the small house
Of Philomel and Baucis at Maphisto's urging
For his throne. So what bargain can enhance

Exchange of skill for skull, of skull for skill,
And broker metamorphosis if not its own?
If own it not? Jupiter and Mercury gave
Philomel and Baucis linden for their love but
Totenkopf sang grave Maphisto's *Lied.*

Old Men Weeping

Old men weeping, wrote the young man
Thinking of the elders of his kin
Of Robert, John, and Dick and Sam,

Skin loose on brittle bones, with thin
Faces, shuffling feet, arthritic joints
And has-been thoughts of might-have-been.

Robert was the first to disappoint
Himself and disappoint as well his friends.
The young man, poet now, appoints

Himself the expert in the means & ends
Of things, including the dark fate
Of John's untoward ambitions and intends

To publish widely, to reveal the hate
His brother's love turned into when he wept
That loss of his position among late

And early rivals both who stepped
Before him when he tried to seize the day.
Dick himself was one of these, and kept

The mantle for himself until his way
Was thwarted by his cousin Sam
Who knew his feet were made of clay

And saw him weep for the young poet
Who was now no longer young.
His book on weeping tanked, although it

Showed how he himself had clung
To drowning older kin
When what he wrote maliciously about them

Rounded on himself and pulled him in.

Collioure and Antonio Machado

Not only the delimited circumferences
but also all the white stone houses
in the streets of southern Catholic cemeteries
speak of walled towns by Vauban
or by his foretypes in the Middle Ages or before.
This silent town within the town of Collioure
where Derain and Picasso paid their bills
with paintings no one wanted yet
fortifies itself against the naked bathers
and the tourists at the Templiers.
I intrude upon the silent tenants searching
for Antonio Machado.

The wealthy dead inhabit their expensive homes
and wait impatiently for quick descendants
to arrive and fill each empty room marked reservée.
The poor lie down in dresser drawers stacked high
in marble walls around a central Calvary
and whisper without any *nouvelle fierte a ce pays:*
"Nous etions vraiment une seule famille."

Machado fled from Franco's armies
first to Barcelona, then across the border
with some refugees. Dying, he came
on foot, and in the rain, and with his mother.
He left the room they gave him only once
to walk alone along the streets of Collioure
before they brought him here.
He sings these dead his mortal words forever.
Globo del fuego . . . disco morado . . .

The sun that parched the bones
dries up the town, dries up the southern sea.
Savilla is distant and alone.
Sol. Soleil.
Castile, and Collioure! Machado.

After A.M.

I loved the house
Where she lived—
Once a magnificent structure of bricks
Now collapsing through
The skeleton of black decaying
Wood that held it up,
Mortar loose and crumbling.

Moonlight pours down on me.
Her own clear light in dreams that make
The windows shine. Badly dressed and sad,
I walk alone along the ancient street.

*

What a luminous evening!
The air itself is enchanted.
The white stork sleeps
As it flies
And the swallows dip over and under each other
On pointed wings
And golden is the wind in which they fly
Dreaming in the happy dusk.

*

The Pythagorean lyre
Continues to hum in the silence
And the rainbow in sunlight's
The same that enters

My stereoscope, even though
I can't quite make it work.
Heraclitus' fire has left ashes
That put out my eyes, and
The world we inhabit right now
Is transparent, empty, blind, & flown.

*

One clear day the wind called to my heart
With the sweet scent of jasmine.

"For this gift," said the wind, "I ask in return
All the scent of your loved and secret roses."
"But I have no roses now, there are no flowers
Left in my garden. All of them died."

"Then give me water from your fountains
And all the dried-up leaves and petals."
The wind left and I wept. And I said to my
Heart, "Corazón, what have you done

With the garden I left you to tend?"

Poems without Pictures[1]

1. It Was Said (text seeking photograph)

Ekstasis—it was said—or was that
ekphrasis—? A lean meme of X or Y
explains all nothings coming at
you going in to stand unstill: Why

not say you exit in those words
instead of only looks—? Still stand-
ing, step away and lean in towards
a henge of stone and with thin wand

go wreck or wound whatever magic
into majesty. It's in your only hand.
Beside yourself and feeling tragic,
You amaze us even without mind-

ing or amending—any bloody one.
Come, come! said Mr. It Was Said.
I'll word your silent image, loan
You stasis, phrasic in your narrow bed.

2.

I'm told by a friend that the early
American poet John Greenleaf Whittier
Would leave—what else?—a green leaf
On a friend's porch or mailbox to announce
That He had made a visit and found an

1 Originally written to accompany the photographs of my daughter, Laura Bendoly, in *Sight Lines* (Dos Madres, 2022). It is here necessary for the reader to imagine pictures of his own that might accompany the poems.

Empty house. It also indicated that he
Would return another day. Friends
Kept these leaves as bookmarks.
Here is a green leaf. It marks the
Beginning of a book.

3.

Whose grim workings
Belch smoke on the western horizon?
Death Valley's not far off.
Near where Arizona and Utah meet
Once the Navaho land was green and living
On the banks of Lake Powell.
Water recedes here and on the Colorado.
No rain falls. Yet some limping thing,
Whether rodent or bird, must
Scratch its dirty claws on this
Parched and dying earth in order to live.

4.

Daisies and hydrangeas
shine both near and far—
near as our spring garden where
they follow snowdrops

by a month, and far as the Netherlands
in the age of Dutch masters who
made still-lives live and breathe
and occupy an otherwise black vacancy.

And the limes? Even farther away—
A store of them aboard
a ship at sea: squeezed by sailors
for their juice against the scurvy,

but also placed with care
on ship's dining table &
admired for their dark green
and slightly irregular shapes

5.

This tree, stripped of branches, was used in
Waiting for Godot and then
Replanted here.
Eventually new branches grew.
But the tree remembered
Its brief life as an actor.
If you come up close and whisper
Je ne suis pas d'ici, monsieur,
It will drop all its leaves,
Call for snow, and wave its many
Bare limbs in anger, saying
I'm not from around these parts myself!

6.

Mimesis is a meta kind of thing
As in met a redwing blackbird
On my walk

Met a gray squirrel
Met a beaver
Met a man walking there, absorbed

7.

Rothko woke up a little groggy & painted
The first of his bright horizontal rectangles
As a vertical instead. What a mistake!
When it then leaked orange all over the
Phone wires, the distant mountains,
And, tending to yellow, also the sky, he
Had achieved accidentally his horizontals and
Was pleased. What a way to begin the day!

8.

Imagine the line of trees in summer.
Just two pines retain their green.
Has all life gone to live beneath them?

If I were lost in all of this negation
I would plod to the pines and ask
Warm animals burrowed there
Among their roots to admit me.

9.

What kind of factory's that
It seems so brutal does it
Smash boulders like the man
Is sitting on to make perhaps

Cement or gravel to build with?
The man's not thinking about
The factory; he's been reading
Yeats and thinking of the past.
He's just looked up from the
Lines where the poet wrote . . .

10.

A Christo-like intervention in red
From which the imagination has already
Taken a swan dive off the end into
The infinite and survived.
But you don't think so. You don't think
It's a stairway to heaven either, but
Just a cobbled together set of steps for
Dull-witted tourists to climb in order
To stand at the top and look at the view.

11.

O Bright façade!

Builder, bolder of Bildungsroman
Might materials gleem

Á la clé, á la Klee may be

To let it shine
Shine oh let it shine

Too sheer to climb, mountaineer!

"No man fathomed"

Or to swim

You'd drown in all that blue

12.

If you were Basho, Issa;
If you were Buson—
You'd find your Haiku in this stream

13.

Horn blast of orange from
The brass section of a hidden orchestra—
And skitterings of woodwinds
At its edges

14.

I am the mimesis tree.
Would you imitate my life?
You think I have none now,
But you are wrong.

I've had enough representation.
Perhaps I'll be a weapon
Or a tool. I dare you to come back
In the summer.

I could wreck your camera with
A single blow. I could tie you up,
Your arms a V on my branches,
You could imitate my pain.

15

If my canvas were asphalt & black
I'd paint white lines—
Maybe a yellow, a red.
Straight ones mostly, resembling
Those that drivers leave behind
When they flee with a quick
Right turn to go left to get out
In the night. The remainder are captives.
And I'd think of a poet I knew
Whose Finlay was concrete
With abhorrence of tar
And who wrote: *Oh*
Liner   *Longliner*   *Lonelier*

16.

Rockface over cave mouths
Painted by Pollock in a blackdog mood?
Yet notice the luminous band
Of translucent green.
If you had strong arms and a light touch

You might be tempted to surf
The green into a cave.
But how would you come out

If you went in? As a cold kiln's
Fiery hypothesis of ice.

17.

If you seek to freeze the moment
Realize the moment melts
To quanta of perception—all men here
You'd say—a gray head, a bald head,
A beard—quickly blurring at indeterminate
Painterly pace. Verticals and horizontals
Are stable enough, but not human. They're
Aspects of the structure of the room.
What are the three young men doing
Who appear to be at the far side of
A coffee bar? Gray, bald, and beard are
Seated at tables, perhaps served by one
Of the younger men. But that was
A while ago. And what do you mean
By served? And what did you mean before
When you asked what they were doing?
How do you do? the Brits say upon meeting.
But I think this is an all-American melt.

18.

Do the walkers humanize the scene?
Or are they dehumanized as part
Of a scenic whole? What would they
Say if you asked them? What

Would Wallace Stevens say? Or Robert Frost?
Would it be different if there were only
One of them? Or if they were both made of salt?

19.

Badland boys early up and
On the road in the spirit
Of modified Kerouac whose
Spirit might have spent the night
Near Sheephole Valley Wilderness
Or maybe at the Anza Borrego Park.
It's a couple of hours before dawn
And the mountains are indifferent
To their rush and rant. But maybe
That's not who they are. Maybe
It's a yawning mother taking her
Daughter to the first music lesson
Of the day. The old woman who
Once played in Paris likes to start
Early. If you approach her small
House in the hills and it's still dark
You hear the piano, or perhaps
You see her waiting on her porch
As the sun begins to rise.

20.

Verde, verde! he cried in his poem
And I would speak that green from
A blue house that isn't mine but blue's.
He cried in the language of Andalucía

Where I've never been but have loved
The green poem that its poet—
Juan Ramon Jimenez—offered to
The fresh green air through
Which a green maiden quietly passed.
"The blues," we say, thinking
Of sadness or jazz. And then we think
Of the sky perhaps or the sea.
Who could ask for more than
A blue house in a green field under
Friendly clouds? Oh, and maybe
A red front door, kept always open.

21.

Low clouds now
Don't quite force the issue
Would fog?
                    Would the drizzle
Of a Nun's November?

22.

In the shade of the oldest tree
Were old men weeping.
On the bright and sunny side
Were young men laughing.

What were the young men laughing at?
Why did the old men weep?
The young men laughed at the old.
The old men wept for the young.

Inside the oldest tree something sang.
The leaves fell down like human tears;
The bare limbs shook and shook
As if with human laughter. Young men

Gathered up the leaves and built a pyre.
Old men formed a circle higher
In the air than young men ever choired.
Then they lit the fire

Ballad of the Three Friends

(After Lorca)

Peter
Vladeta
Göran

Only once together in my garden.
Peter Michelson, the big American.
Vladeta Vuckovic, the swarthy Serb.
Göran Printz-Påhlson, the pale Swede.

Peter
Vladeta
Göran

Peter blocking Big Daddy Lipscomb with
A forearm shiver
Trying out for the Chicago Bears.
Vladeta in the hills with Tito's Partisans
Looking down in the misty valley
through binoculars.
Göran in his uniform beside the Bofors Gun
Declaring himself to be Socialist
And scoffing at his orders.

Peter
Vladeta
Göran

Peter in Chicago as a student
reading William Burroughs in a secret attic.
Vladeta in Nazi-held Vienna

Writing on recursive functions
And an allied spy
Among the local prostitutes.
Göran leaving Sweden
To become an Englishman and speak
A better English than the Brits.

Peter
Vladeta
Göran

Peter writing his *Pacific Plainsong*
Reading it aloud
To students in an auditorium
The night I met him.
Vladeta handing in his thesis
Shaking up the world of mathematics
For a year or so.
Göran drinking with his pal von Sydow
Telling him how much
He didn't like the Bergman films.

Peter
Vladeta
Göran

Peter with me in Grant Park the year
Chicago cops smashed the heads
And tear-gassed the faces
Of our students there.
Vladeta unwilling to be Yugoslav
Wanting only to be Serbian

The year we co-translated *Kosovo.*
Göran drinking pints of beer
While holding forth on Strindberg
In a Cambridge pub.

Peter
Vladeta
Göran

Peter with his fat round face leaning down
To bless us in my garden
With his laugh and smile.
Vladeta beside him saying come to Belgrade
And we'll drink together
Glasses full of local wine and brandy.
Göran saying to them both
We'll sing together at the festival
In Stockholm and I'll see
You both receive the Nobel Prize

Peter
Vladeta
Göran

Peter growing old in Boulder Colorado
Calling me to say goodbye
Dying in a small expensive nursing home.
Vladeta infuriated by my poem
For Sarajevo under siege
Longing for a Kosovo for Serbs
And cutting me in public
Before disappearing wholly

For the last months of his life.
And Göran falling down the stairs
After swigging bog myrtle schnapps
Following a reading back in Malmö.

Ballad for the three friends

Peter
Vladeta
Göran

Göran, Vladeta, and Peter
Three friends
Laughing once with me in my summer garden
Laugh no more
Nor feel the heat of the sun
Bajo el cri cri cri de las pájaros negros.

Under the cry cry cawing of the crows.

OldSingSung

I'll take what ill befell
That belfry said me eld
Billiam, scat-rhyme
Fellow hilltop hiker-cat.
The church was empty,
Long abandoned by
Parishioner and priest.
Long abandoned by its
Pews and pulpit too.
The belfry had been
Struck by lightning, & so
Everybody fled, and not
Just for a day, and not
Just for the May, O welladay.
Sings Bill—that old bloke
Forgotten by the local folk—
A holyholly hymnkin.
He's a-showing me
Around his oldest haunts
As hedabeen a local aince.
Lookitfell and then it settled.
You can't see it, but it
Shadow rhymes with kettle.

From Gösta Frieberg's "The Growing": Conclusion

. . . Oh. benign & generous Powers . . .

. . . Protect the magic parts of the earth,
Forests, oceans . . .

. . . Protect the daylight whose invisible energies
Vanish in waves across the tops of trees.
If there were nothing to meet them from below
They would continue straight on downwards
In enormous blackness . . .

*

The entirely beautiful
Tiny face of the ant
Next to a spruce needle . . .
And she takes hold of the needle, coaxing
Its green splendor to its place . . .

                    On its back,
Carries it home.

*

    The earth's
    Faintly glowing
    Egg
    On a leaf.   And the glowworm
Curved around it—like the weak, faraway
    Light from our galaxy—

    The giving-of-birth.

(Trans. from the Swedish with Göran Printz-Påhlson)

Reverdy's Farewell

A glowing that's beyond the head
A bounding heart

On the hill where the air tests its voice

The rays of a wheel
The sun in its course

At a crossroads
By the small hill

a prayer

A few words that nobody hears

Closer to the sky

And on its steps
the last square of light

(Trans. from the French of Pierre Reverdy, with Catherine Perry)

• Part II •

(*a Draft of XXX Sonnets in Prose*)

A Draft of XXX Sonnets
(in Prose)
or
the Étienne-Hillish-Hejinian Variations

i.m. Stanley Rosen, Philosopher

I

Two women, French and American, wrote books that respect the fourteen lines of the sonnet but omit meter and rhyme. The line can be short or very long, if you still call that a line. Are they still sonnets? Only sort of. *Only sort of suits me.*

Oxota: A Short Russian Novel by Lyn Hejinian was published in 1991 by "The Figures." *King of a Hundred Horsemen* by Marie Étienne was published *en face* with the French in Marilyn Hacker's translation by FSG in 2008. I'm drawing on their methods here. All three are hereby conscripted and inscribed.

I'm also drawing on my friend Geoffrey Hill's *The Book of Baruch by the Gnostic Justin*. I say "my friend." Ha. I knew him a little long ago. Hill doesn't restrict himself to fourteen-line passages, but he writes in the same spirit as Étienne and Hejinian. His "lines" are sometimes longer than any of theirs. You could call this Hill's "late style."

Think of all the rigorous true sonnets written by Hill.

The thirteen sonnets of "Lachrimae, or Seven Tears figured in seven Passionate Pavans" are his best in the Petrarchan mode. But the blank verse sonnets of "Funeral Music" are still the ones I like best.

They simply take your breath away. (What a cliché.)

Hill loosened up when he came to America and took SSRIs for his depression. He revealed this himself in an interview. Can one call *The Triumph of Love, Speech! Speech!,* and *The Orchards of Syon* "drug induced"?

Not really. Oh, maybe *Speech! Speech!*

I imagine I take more drugs than he did. More about that later.

I don't know if Lyn Hejinian or Marie Étienne took any drugs.

Lyn Hejinian signed *Oxota* for me in 1996. She signed it "Love, from Lynn," though I don't think she really loved me. I was meeting her for the first time. I have never met Marie Étienne or Marilyn Hacker. The blurb says that *King of a Hundred Horsemen* involves "a complex but playful reinterpretation of the sonnet form and moves from the jungles of Indochina to the Atlanta airport."

I've never been in the jungles of Indochina.

But I've been lost in the mazes of the Atlanta airport.

This is line fourteen.

II

Hillish, not Hellish. You may have missed that. Early on he references both his difficulties figuring taxes owed for, it must be, whatever year corresponds to the composition of his section 99, and his "logical dyslexia."

Regarding the latter, does he mean just formal logic? The kind taught by philosophers like our mutual friend Stanley Rosen? Or does he mean he just gets all messed up in a sentence like a dyslexic kid who, basically, can't read at all. Certainly that's not the case. He can even write. But we'll just let it stand, along with the problem of dating the sections of this long poem.

Hellish enough is our realization that Hillish *speech!speech!* in the book is intended to end only with his own death. He would not, he *did* not, see the book into print. Sections were sent in the mail to Kenneth Haynes, who took them in the order received and made the book. So Hill knew he was writing posthumous work.

Kenneth Haynes is writing his biography. It's quite possible that the lives of Marie Étienne, Marilyn Hacker, and Lyn Hejinian would be more interesting than Hill's, and therefore make for better biographies. Hill was a dusty scholar type, burning his candle at just one end. It was Edna St. Vincent Millay who burned her candle at both ends, or said she did. Lyn, Marie, and Marilyn led and still are leading more cosmopolitan lives not always in the context of the Pedagogical Imperative. (Don't forget that problem with taxman. If he'd not taught at Leeds and Cambridge and Oxford and Boston he'd just pay a working stiff's minimum. His student Tony Harrison actually has "poet" where it asks for a profession on a UK passport.

Is poetry a profession?

A line can have as few as just four words.

Or just three.

Or two.

One.

Hill says he has become “approximate” and “hexed.” Then he says he finds that “shamming.” Upon which realization he’s prone to “slip into something comfortable, such as self-harming.” Indeed he says “the crassest form of self-harm, that I have long practiced, is the poem.”

That doesn’t make the writing of poems sound like a profession.

And yet he was even Oxford Professor of Poetry.

The job’s not entirely honorary, but it’s badly paid. His half-deaf friend thought he heard GH exclaim, “I’ve been appointed Oxford Professor of Perjury.”

It’s true; he had.

III

But then everybody lies. Sometimes at least.

Oxota is subtitled: *A Short Russian Novel*, its sonnets meant to rival Pushkin's in E*ugene Onegin*. But it's not written in Russian and it's not a novel. I wonder if Hejinian read Vikram Seth's *The Golden Gate*, published five years before her *Oxota*. It's a real narrative, it's a sequence of real rhyming sonnets, it's more Pushkin than any King of any Hundred Horsemen might have been in French.

And I can relate to its Acknowledgments:

My debts are manifold and various:
First, Stanford University
Where, with progressively precarious
Nature, my tardy Ph.D.
Has waxed, and waxes, lax and sickly
Second, to friends who've read this, quickly
Advised me to desist and cease,
Or burbled, "What a masterpiece!"

And that's just the octave. *The Golden Gate* really translates Pushkin into Californian, a language spoken in that book by an Indian. Did he ever finish his Stanford PhD? I never finished mine, and once lied that I was on the verge of doing so to get a job. Perhaps lied is too strong a word. I was living in London with my housemate Igor Webb and my soon-to-be bride Diana Adams. She attended the Russian Orthodox Church and studied the Russian language at Holborn College. She read me Pushkin in bed, start to finish, in that phantasmagoric year when everything seemed to be, well, phantasmagoric, as I said (thinking of H. James). We'd go to the Russian Embassy for Stalinist musicals and vodka; we'd watch the old émigrés play chess; we'd go together through the list of questions provided to an applicant wanting a menial position with MI5. In those days her Russian was an asset. No Professor of Perjury like Geoffrey Hill, but still stretching the truth, I told the chair

Via a rare

Transatlantic phone call (June, 1967) that indeed my dissertation was "almost done"

IV

When in fact it was hardly begun. And you can do enjambment even when you're lazy and write your sonnets in prose.

Where was I? Diana. Russian as an asset.

• A useful or valuable quality, person, or thing; an advantage or resource: proved herself an asset to the company.
• A valuable item that is owned.
• A spy working in his or her own country and controlled by the enemy.

That doesn't count as a line. Just putting my cards on the table.

But was Arkadii Dragomoshchenko an asset for Hejinian in *Oxota*? I think so, as she thanks him in a note and quotes him in her Chapter 109. According to the first definition. He was a valuable person and his Russian an advantage and a resource you can be sure, a man with useful qualities. She "owned" him in the sense that she acknowledges his being and his help. I own it too, so help me, that Diana was my own amanuensis now and then, in Russian and in truth. Something analogous you'll find in most Professors of Perjury.

But what about "A spy working in his or her own country and controlled by the enemy." Perhaps the enemy of Russian is my English. Perhaps in Ukraine it is Ukrainian.

(Writing this in 2022 I find we're told by some to stop reading Russian books. You mean we can't have Pushkin, Dostoevsky, Tolstoy? Not without a touch of Putin say the fiercest of the most committed faction.)

As I type this out I'm listening to Valentin Silverstrov's piano works performed by Jenny Lin. His "Duet with Silence" has almost no notes at all. There's a note. Wait, wait, wait, wait, wait, wait, wait, but, but, but . . . and there's at last another. I put the CD on as Silverstrov's Ukranian.

But back to 1991, it seems so long ago.

Quoting by translating and, she says, by mistranslating, Lyn writes as Lin plays a few more recorded notes of the "Duet with Silence" in my room.

And for me, in defiance of the laws governing the despondent progression and movement of days . . .

The unbearably white sun hangs immobilized in a strontium-turquoise dusty sky declining imperceptibly toward some boundary which is too speculative to allow one to differentiate anything from anything else . . .

A juggler is discovered in a church juggling fruits because he has no other "language" . . . and a sense of insane optical clarity alternates with the flashing heat of his hands moving in a predatory measured pace toward some materialization that is like . . .

That is like?

Like when I stood beside Diana in the London Russian Orthodox Church and marveled at her beauty and her grace. It was an Easter service, and one stands throughout. One stands a very long time. I longed for something I could almost reach . . . something I might juggle as I could not speak . . . oranges, perhaps.

V

What Hillish meds did they feed you there in Boston, Geoffrey? I'm surprised that, with your reticence about your private life, you admitted to any at all. There's a Boston poet whose dad I understand was your shrink, and I'm told by an informant (spy?) that you liked his institution well enough that you wanted to stay when they wanted you to go. You enjoyed all the board games and pickleball.

For me, the psych ward felt like being lost in the jungles of Indochina or the mazes of Atlanta's airport: *Entre le peur du bout et elle de maintenant, la hâte extreme de présent, se succèdent les peurs, celles de morts possible.* Between fear of the end and fear of the moment, the terrible swiftness of the present, fears follow on each other, the fears of possible deaths.

Although I didn't die, my wife Diana did. Far away from me and in another's care, as I was no longer fit to serve.

I'd quote something in Russian here but haven't got Cyrillic on my keyboard.

But I can write *Cymbalta, Mirtazapine, Olanzapine, Lorazapam*, and several other words that signified for me no cure. I take them still, though only out of habit. Maybe what I'm typing here's a talking cure.

In your poem to our mutual friend Rosen, you write in "Discourse"

> *Arbeitsknecht*[1] by adoption, I never
> Hurl down advice, even to shake the building . . .
> You're magisterial in judgment's gorge
> Where the rocks are at all angles and the stream
> Huggers its way through . . .

---

1 *Arbeitsknecht*, German: Gruntboy. A Gruntboy is a rugged and exciting young man from the North East of England who is outrageously foul-mouthed and toilet-humoured on the outside but is surprisingly sweet, tender and devoted when he becomes your friend.

Bugger that, I thought when I read it — but then went on to this:

> You're magisterial in your own conviction
> And a clown with it, and a judge of clowns.

VI

Arbeitsknecht! Moi? Personne ne voit personne.

De temps en temps, quelqu'un va jusqu'au fond, on ne s'en remet pas, il a touché, mais quoi?

It's hard to imagine GH posing as a gruntboy, even if Professor Rosen was magisterial in his own conviction and a clown with it. (See footnote to part V.) But first be certain that you've taken all your meds. It's almost a poem if you count it out in lines:

Cymbalta
Mirtazipine
Olanzapine
Lorazapam

There was a time a few months ago when I would try to comfort myself by reciting the poem that was Diana's English home:

Cherry Tree
Hacheston
Woodbridge
Suffolk

Take three of one, half a dozen of the others. I loved the place. Wrote about it many times in poems that worked for me like dowsing rods that hovered over secret wells. They allowed me to imagine green pastures when I was in the gray cities. Even though "the Hebrew is uncertain" I was comforted "in places of repose." I dislike the alternative translation for what follows and think that you will too: "All the fat men of the earth shall eat." What about the thin ones? Sends you back to the King James version even if you're not a royalist.

That second line above: *From time to time, someone goes all the way to the bottom, no one can get over it, he touched something, but what?* "My name is Ang."

VII

My name is Anxiety. Marie Étienne says her name is Ang in *King of a Hundred Horsemen.* But of course it's actually Marie. Lyn's name is Hejinian, and Geoffrey's is Hill. An early poem of his is "God's Little Mountain." I suppose a little mountain is a Hill. Lyn says in Chapter Nineteen that "realism is very optimistic." Is this thing I'm writing "realism"?

Certainly not.

And am I optimistic?

What would you reply, having read this far?

I said *am I optimistic*?

OK, I take your silence for silence. "Silence gives consent" said Thomas Moore, but they cut off his head anyway. Before the headsman swung down his axe he also said: "Don't cut off my beard, for it has not annoyed the King." That's *sprezzatura* for you. But not optimism.

I have a pill-splitter that looks just like a guillotine.

A Spell-Plitter is something you'd only find in a Russian novel where happy families are all alike but unhappy families are unhappy each in its own way. My family, what's left of it, is planning to visit. I am told I must not wear a mask.

Even with co-morbidities. Back when I counted cousins and even second cousins as part of my family I listened to the radio and *Who was that masked man*? *Why he's the Lone Ranger.*

I've always been a bad speller, always needed a plitter and a thicktionario-thesario-ensicklopodium. My family's much reduced and those remaining will take the rapid-antigen test. Hugs will be required. I'm urged to practice

hugging in order "to get back in shape."
    I'm in lousy shape.
    I think I'm shaped as something very like a louse.
    The house of kindred's very much reduced.
    Hindered maybe's the internal rhyme.

VIII

Full rhyme in time.
Do I pray for our poor nation and our miserable selves?
More likely pry.
Into this or that. But I've come to like the Torah
of my Midrash in the Jewish Text Society's edition. Fresh
and new to me after long life with the fruits of King James'
committee. Still, I know when I'm there I'm but a visiting
goy. Like a boy fascinated by his neighbor's house.
What's Revised Standard is the sundered self.
Please use "sundered" in a sentence.
The crunch of bone when it is sundered.

Thunder, then.
One of those drugs I mentioned I'm required to take
off label. It's designed for schizophrenics and psychotics.
Sundered all.
Who's paid to make up the crazy names for new
pharmaceuticals? Is it out of work poets? (All poets are out of
work). Tell you what. Prozac, Avepro: Why not, Zach, have
a pro, have a con. Those I didn't mind, but I can tell you
Olanzapine's a poison. Try it for yourself. They don't advertise
it on TV. Pried open for all the world to see said Mr. B (for
Berryman).
I can reach with my middle fingers to the iRig keys
while still typing on my QWERTY alphabetic, thereby
providing for myself my own musical accompaniment. It's a
stretch to nail the sharps and flats. But muscle memory still
serves. Does that remain if one is Alzheimered out of mind?
The iRig's memory is set to automatically remember
all my improvisations.

May we all be saved—Jews, Gentiles, Johns.

When we lived in Little Shelford outside Cambridge our front door was very wide. Severeal times some ducks walked in, and once even a horse.

IX

Ce suite utilse des cookies et vous donne le controle sur ceux que vous souhaitez active.

Does metaphysics speak in ordinary language and was GH present at Professor Rosen's presentation in his seminar, BU 1996? You don't know Stanley but you like the GH take in "Discourse" anyway. You can Google up an introduction for the plebs at *https://stanleyrosen.jimdofree.com/audio-and-video/?fbclid=IwAR1ZNgQ_3uqMBQ5Ouy8CO3oJaxDDwF707HkcOpTev4Cm8PbSX4tm9Y-4g*.

First C-Span question: "Who was Plato?"

In fact I recommend beginning with "Kojeve's Paris," where the distinguished Jesuit, Father Gaston Fessard, contrasts with Leo Straus. And I recall the nature of a three-way conversation in the GH suite of rooms at Notre Dame, the third besides myself being Joseph Buttigieg, Gramsci scholar, former Jesuit himself, and father of the presidential candidate, the former Mayor Pete.

When GH got the picture he looked in a pained way at Joe saying, "A great loss for the Order."

Orders of the day: Introduce the King of a Hundred Horsemen into the plot of the short Russian novel, *Oxota*. Your Highness, this is Arkadii Dragomo and Zina Dragomo and Ostap Dragomo for short. Welcome to the plot.There is a plot? You discover it the same way you outfox Heidegger, with "ordinary language" in a struggle with The Dialectic.

"The plot of *Oxota*'s a big nothing seems to me."

Not so fast there, Geoffrey. In Russki it can mean "Hunt," and isn't *The Book of Baruch by the Gnostic Justin* also on a hunt, in "ordinary language" that eludes the estrangements seeking nothing, I mean *Nothing*, in the "ordinary experience" of philosophers?

Who's to transmit the ancient wisdom into a contemporary terrain, say the terrain of *Oxota* through. . . ?

. . . the ordinary experience of *doksa*, not advocating a recuperation of *phronêsis* at the expense of *ratio* and *technê*? This being the context for the claim that it is possible to think Nothing. Not about Nothing. No about aboutness. No empty mind either. Can we talk about things without referring to them? "I have nothing to say and I am saying it and that is poetry," said John Cage. But what is philosophy?

There are no rules for the application of rules.

This is not a sonnet in an ordinary sense.

This is not a notness either.

The philosopher was asked what he was thinking about, and he said "Oh, nothing," sounding like Pooh Bear. And then he hit the road to *Oxota*.

X

Phronêsis is a jazz trio, formed in 2005 by Danish bass player Jasper Høiby. The piano trio is completed by British pianist Ivo Neame and Swedish drummer Anton Eger.

Are you eager, Anton, too eager—ahead of the beat?
Is Ivo playing tritone intervals in the heat
Of Jasper's plonking base and thumping feet?.

Stanley Rosen liked beautiful women
My wife Diana was a beautiful woman
Therefore Rosen liked my wife

And called her "Diana Strangeways." That I never understood and thought it must be some private joke between the philosopher and Diana. Even a Google search only links Diana (the late UK Princess) and a Strangeways family, but that's not the kind of ordinary experience that he referenced and recommended to GH.

Associations are not free. Free association is about as free as a sequence of syllogisms.

It's the truth.

But what we're doing in this Hillish-Étienne-Hejinian is associational. Did I say that when we lived in Little Shelford outside Cambridge our front door was very wide? Several times some ducks walked in, and once even a horse.

Does *Phronêsis* sometimes manage a fugato?
In the future perfect
Will have managed a fugato, thank you very much.

XI.
Little Fugato. (Order: LH, ME, GH)

This time we are both.

The puzzle existed, I hoped gradually to put its pieces back in place. scattered by what fright?

Rehearse the autopsy: Psyche cut as ever. Not clever. Cute, my arse.

The old thaw is inert, everything set again in snow

If anyone asked me, so many years spent writing, does that make any sense? I could try to answer, to explain.

Gross antennae of abstruse *monnaie*. Grand opera phony did you say?

At insomnia, at apathy.

I have a taste for dates and a sense of debt, I am there to bear witness.

Nascent fissures, indecent pressures; thong askew, thing into thing; I ask you.

We must learn to endure the insecurity as we read.

Our quest will cease when we arrive at our point of departure, knowing the spot for the first time.

Unpleasant sly origins barely decent. Brythonic goddess of panic still on the margins. Explains my odes.

The felt need for a love intrigue.

Obviously writing is a return, a supplement to a journey.

XII.
Little fugato reversed:
Approx. Dodecophons for the left hand

Or would it be better like this?

Obviously writing is a return, a supplement to a journey.

The felt need for a love intrigue.

Unpleasant sly origins barely decent. Brythonic goddess of panic still on the margins. Explains my odes.

Our quest will cease when we arrive at our point of departure, knowing the spot for the first time.

We must learn to endure the insecurity as we read.

Nascent fissures, indecent pressures; thong askew, thing into thing. I ask you.

I have a taste for dates and a sense of debt. I am there to bear witness

At insomnia, at apathy.

Gross antennae of abstruse *monnaie*. Grand opera phony did you say?

If anyone asked me, so many years spent writing, does that make any sense?

The old thaw is inert, everything set again in snow.

Rehearse the autopsy: Psyche cut as ever. Not clever. Cute, my arse.

The puzzle existed. I hoped gradually to put its pieces back in place scattered by what fright?[1]

---

1 Becaue I made "Or would it be better like this" the first line, we have, alas, a widow still remaining: "This time we are both." But I have had plans for that line for some time, so why not begin the next part with it and cut to the chase?

XIII

This time we are both.

Thing is, you see, halfway through the Étienne Ang suddenly becomes Lam. In that sense I suppose "we" are both Ang and Lam. Lam is both a king and, it would seem, the director of a kind of theater performed in his mind before a participating audience. I begin to fear the old tropes.

Shakespeare, etc.

This little world, etc.

C'est la fin qui précède et le début qui suit.

Simple, that. You can translate for yourself. *Autrement dit, pour étre, il faut avoir été.* You have to *été* before you can *être*. You have to eat before you have eaten. No, no; that's not it. When my mother first met Diana, she was surprised that this young woman with an upper-class British accent said she had "already *et*," talking like a hillbilly. I told her that was British usage, that Diana would never say she had "already eaten." She went to the dictionary and showed me: "See," she said, "Regional: *et*. It's a polite way of saying hillbilly." "Look again," I said: and she did. "British: *et*." And continued reading: "eat one's words," and "eat one's heart out," and "perform fellatio upon."

Mistranslation as follows of Étienne, Section 72 regarding the responses to Lam's performance in his mind:

Doesn't matter a damn, old boy, them beginnings like the ends is already set and established in the disorders of order, so fuck it.

You die first, then jump about like a headless chicken till you end up in the pot like a cooked goose.

You come back before you go away, put yourself into circulation, get acquainted with the fact that it all happens at once.

You're early or you're late same difference says Ang as part of the audience or is she just Lam-basted with the rhetoric and blackbird in a π

Pi is 3.14159 but you save that for dessert.

Every moment of every life: same time, same thing.

Mix up yours and mine all in the dust of time.

XIV

Re-vision of *Oxota* from Hungarian translation into Indiana English including a paragraph from Mrs. Adams' *Young George* all about the first movement of the French at Waterloo—

Reading Étienne in Hungarian feels something like this:

When the smoke lifted, all English eyes turned to the hill around Belle Alliance. From there came a roar of cheers as a great column of men started to advance, and it seemed as if part of the hillside itself had broken away and was sliding down towards the valley below.

Mrs. Adams was Diana's mother. The Battle of Waterloo was eventually won for the English by the Duke of Wellington and his men. But imagine how that sliding hillside might have felt translated into Hungarian.

Therefore we revise.

Young George was Mrs. Adams' sixteen-year-old ancestor from the Keppel family archive and genealogy.

She writes of him in English, staring at the French. But imagine all of this coming at you in Hungarian.

Oxota: You can't find it wending in translation when it's wondering in Indiana in the hands of democratic citizens. The only trans types allowed are the translators. Russian is a natural for a "short Russian novel," but Hungarian? It's only spoken by Hungarians.

Hungry enough, and verbatim: *Poetry is violent.*

The meanings of words annihilate each other.

De Sade only imitates writing in all the acts that he describes.

Our comments fall into different semantics.

Philosophical, anecdotal, and intimate.

You could repeat it several times.

XV

But why *Baruch*? A means of revision into Metaphysics of Ordinary language? I don't think *Oxota's* metaphysical. Is Geoffrey? Is Professor Rosen?

A question certainly to pose in class: *Whose* Ordinary Language? It would seem to be a question begged.

Before you bagged your goose for the pot that calls the kettle black.

Can you say that in Hungarian? In Russian? Is Ordinary Language ordinary in International Cuisine? Is a hillside standing up and coming at you like a wave?

Some regard *Baruch* as part of *Jeremiah*. Its author either way "The Gnostic Justin." But it depends: Do you speak Ordinary Greek or Ordinary Hebrew?

Are you *Septuagint* or are you *Masoretic*?

If you're good enough at Gnosticism you'd revise *Oxota* into metaphysics.

At least you'd find it possible.

But you'd keep things secret as to sacred. The Professor says: *Thinking is as such concealment: to be is to dissimulate*. Was GH in Stanley Rosen's seminar?

I've asked this before. I may ask it again.

He sees "a moving army of metaphors, metonymies, anthropomorphisms" coming at him like a furious Mrs. Adams with that moving hillside in her hand as if it were a rolling pin.

Someone has to do the dishes. I can't remember quite who wrote the line "Weeping into the washing-up." But that's what happens if you try to do the dishes and continue conversation from the dinner table.

About metaphysics.

I've got the plates and silver that the three of us
— Diana, her mum, and I — washed up there in Suffolk
now translated to my house in South Bend, Indiana.

XVI

Too many Baruchs! Him of the official Apocrypha, or of the Greek Apocalypse, or the Syriac—translated from a Greek original (lost)—not to mention the so-called "Rest of the Words of Baruch," the mention in Jeremiah (J's loyal scribe) and a Latin Baruch cited, with quotes, but otherwise missing. The leading scholar of all this tells me that our guy, the Gnostic Baruch, appears in "The Rest of the Words."

Here I have a brief vision of GH in his garden in his 80th year pondering the same problem. Was GH himself a Gnostic? That would be hard to prove. But certainly he was 80, as I am now—same age as Paul McCartney, Bob Dylan, and Brian Wilson: Birthdays celebrated as I sing my sonnets writ in prose.

The Syriac Baruch stayed behind to sing laments when God sent tribes of Jews to Babylon. GH wrote a book called *Canaan*. Is his *Baruch* to *Canaan* as Canaan Land itself, recalled by prophets left in wrecked Jerusalem with Jews in Babylonian captivity, might be to Blake's vision of Jerusalem hovering in Hill's ruined England once a green and pleasant land? Dylan, Wilson, and McCartney could sing a triaged requiem for that, and for themselves, and for my own sorry self at eighty. So here's from the Syriac for Bobby, Paul, and Brian:

For the youth of the world is past.
And the strength of creation already exhausted.
And the advent of the times is very short.
And the pitcher is near to the cistern.
And the ship to the port.
And life to its consummation.

So who's the Walrus, who's the Carpenter? Where's the Surfer Girl and Mr. Tambourine-Man? I'm not sleepy and there is no place I'm going to.

Are you like a rolling stone? I am.
Are you all alone? You are.

Embrace the Syriac Baruch.
But do not covet Gnosis.

XVII

Three of four Baruchs stagger off the page into Stanley Rosen's living room. He's already grown impatient talking to me about Oxota. He's been busy with his interrogation of the Gnostic Justin. Asked him to indicate "The Correct Baruch." But now I've got him sidetracked. In Oxota they regard him not as a philosopher but merely as a professor of philosophy.

Do philosophers hear voices? Brian Wilson did. Heard music too.

Stanley drowns out everything by turning up the volume of his sound system after placing Mozart's *Requiem* in the machine. Mozart certainly heard voices, and they sang. No one's singing here or in Oxota yet. But there's lots of talk and all the speakers have turned their volumes up in order to compete with Mozart.

When Diana had her Parkinson's hallucinations she would look at me and say: There are three John Matthiases, and you're not a single one of them. There are more Baruchs than just three. I see yet another one attempting to hide behind Stanley's mammoth woofer. That's a kind of speaker in his system, not a dog. It's for the way down notes, the southern notes, the dark ones. The whole house shakes in the *Dies Irae*. I guess we must be gathered for the seminar, and GH is presenter for tonight. Or that's how I imagine it. But I'm surprised that Stanley's room is in Oxota. That I never guessed.

GH talks about obsessive subjects, mumbles in D minor, K.626.

GH has seven cats, all called Seamus Heaney.

They had foreknowledge that Bob Dylan would win

the Nobel Prize, but insisted that foreknowledge doesn't mean predestination. It was always possible to win the bloody thing for themselves

The focus of his presentation is the Blitz. He has childhood memories of Ed Murrow's broadcasts and Praise-Singer's songs. Sin-eater. Rain-bringer. Down go those Wren churches in The City. St. Paul's somehow saved. For background to the war he invokes the General Strike. The Deep State is Tudor, its poets Jonson, Donne & Co. He "sees" the veritable Elohim ensconced in the north, admits to panic attacks, primitive fears, the acrostics of the Gnostics. Only then does he invoke "Baruch by the Book" and the "ablative dead."

From Deep State emerge also John Dee, Inigo Jones, and Justice Coke bearing with him laws and Lawes.

Rabbi Ben Ezra's with him too, and has this song to sing:

Lawses and Jenkyns guard they rest
Dolmetssch ever be thy guest.

But Mozart overwhelms the "viol's wood" of this cacophony, and Stanley grows professional.

He must in the end give us all a grade for this course and we're not bloody well speaking his bleeding Ordinary Language.

XVIII

Justin's *Baruch* arrives by e-mail attachment from GnosticHaven.com, a former Chautauqua near Petoskey, Michigan. (Nothing there but thousands of little sparks.) Anyway, there's a Father of all begotten things who mates with a girl called Eden. Father is our old pal Elohim. Over everything rules The Good, known to believers as GadZooks.edu. Paradise was for the happiness of Elohim and his girlfriend Ms. Eden. And they beget some angels, one of which is our Baruch. There's an evil angel called Nass. Nass the badass. But Baruch has a serious talk with Moses, and another one with Jesus. And so it goes. But I don't really think that GH believed in all this stuff, though with Stanley Rosen, he may have thought of thinking, philosophy, and poetry as implying secrets, even when expressed in Ordinary Language.

Whew. Glad to be through with all of that.

While I've been looking for Baruch Lyn has gone on walking through Oxota. She did not sign up for Stanley Rosen's seminar, but maybe one by the Russian poet, briefly mentioned earlier, he with the longest name of all the hacks belonging to the writer's union, though he himself was not a hack. Wikipedia has a little speaker icon by the name which speaks it loudly with aplomb:

Arkadii Trofimovich Dragomoshchenko.

He too is on the march with Lyn, though there are many stops along the way where the two relax with other writers, hangers on, and Russian types that one has met in Dostoyevsky and Bulgakov. The latter has the best writers' union scenes.

Anyway, Arkadii taught philosophy at the Petersburg State University.

And somehow, somewhere he met Lyn Hejinian.

Oxota spends a lot of time in cramped apartments with the usual communal kitchens and bathrooms when one would like to be out on the open road.

This was all before Putin. It was in the time of Soviet Glasnost

***Oxót** jemú zanimát'sja étim?!*—What makes him do it?!

1 Hunt 2 Chase 3 Go Shooting

All good questions. Topics for the Dragomoshchenko seminar. Oxota, I would say, is both the destination and the journey. *Oxota* Obiter Dicta:

You are the proximity of your own persistence.

Poetry isn't beauty, it's inquiry.

If there are no great opposites there are no great parallels.

XIX

"There's abundant narrative content, but anecdotes and events are presented in non-linear form, since they unfolded over extended periods of time and thus came to Hejinian's attention piecemeal. *Oxota* (which means variously "huntress," "hunt," and "desire" in Russian) is a novel in which contexts, rather than contents, are kept in the foreground."

Huntress, Hunt, Desire. The Amazon blurber used a Russian dictionary two thirds different from mine.

But my notion that *Oxota* is both the destination and the process of getting there is still confirmed. Will the blurb sell books? Probably not.

The Huntress Desires to Hunt. Or, Desire brings the Huntress to the Hunt. Where Hunt is a place, a destination. In the present. In the present tense. Shall I meet you at The Hunt? Is that where the Huntress expresses her Desire? Is there sex in this Pushkinesque novel? A duel in which the hero kills his friend. Where an ingenue dances with a rich sophisticate, writes him a letter, falls in love, is abandoned. Where the H of things becomes a C? *Whoso list to hunt.*

The erotic element will lead from the Dragomoshehenko seminar to the Rosen, from Leningrad to Boston. Arkadii himself ended up a US prof. Did he and Stanley pass each other on the street without a greeting? Arcadii died here, not in Oxota. So did Yevtushenko of the empty stadiums. Further obiter dicta:

> *The feeding of everyday life is put to sex.*
> *There's no need to distinguish a poem from prose.*
> *The mere mood of our words produces content.*

Can they meet each other—Lyn, Arcadii, Yevtushenko, Stanley—in the present tense if nobody believes in presence. Are these words a presence? Are you? Is Geoffrey Hill?

The dead are always with us.

The head of a penis feels like velvet in a mouth.

Fourteen lines have eros as their mystic member.

They change the H to C for Cunt.

If push comes to Pushkin, you're an 80 year old pornographer.

XX

Is Pushkin present with Arcadii and Lyn in Oxota the place? The novel is said to be Pushinesque. But presence is always a problem. Am I present to you? Are you present to me? Are we both present standing before *Oxota* while Arcadii, Lyn, and Puskin are in it? Stanley thinks we secrete the present as a spider does a spiderweb. It's a question of praxis. And ultimately of eros. I produce my present time as I act, as I write.

Pushkin's present time was ended in a duel. Is he conjured back in *Onegin's* Russian stanzas? In Johnston's English versions? In Nabokov's? Does he live in Lyn's fleeting references? In mine?

In Chapter Fifty-One *A pipe in Pushkin's house has popped.*

It sings.

Is Pushkin's house *Onegin* or a place that tourists visit in Saint Petersburg?

Would a broken pipe in Pittsburgh sound the same?

Book II of *Oxota* includes subtitles as well as section numbers: *Innocence, Conspiracy, Passion, Suffering, Betrayal, Death, Redemption.*

All pertaining in one way or another to Pushkin.

Is Pushkin present in *Golden Gate* by Seth
Because the *Onegin* stanza's used?

I'm young, employed, healthy, ambitious
Sound, solvent, self-made, self-possessed.
But all my symptoms are pernicious
The Dow-Jones of my heart's depressed.

XXI

The sunflower of my youth is wilting.
The tower of my dreams is tilting.
The zoom lens of my zest is blurred.
The drama of my life's absurd
What is the root of my neurosis?
I jog, eat brewer's yeast each day,
And yet I feel life slip away.
I wait your sapient diagnosis.
I die! I faint! I fail! I sink!
"You need a lover, John, I think."

Well, that was fun.

But written in another age. Have I lost anyone? Double file, get into the crocodile. Lyn and Arcadii; Geoffrey and Stanley; Justin and Baruch; Marie and Marilyn; Alexander and Eugene; and by himself Mikhail.

Who is Mikhail, you'd ask.

He's Mikhail Bulgakov and he's decided to tag along. He's looking for a stranger who's accompanied by a sinister black cat the size of a fattened pig. Quick now. Hurry along everybody.

XXII

It's hard to stay in line where days of glasnost and perestroika make a text composed by those two songs sound elegiac.

There's a colonel who comes and goes. Does he live in the flat?

And how long will the lecture be once we file in?

The lecturer is Maxim Kantor, novelist and painter. He seems to speak in anecdotes. Adults and children take their places. He begins.

"And when the American philanthropists got excited about the new Russian reforms a group of them sent to impoverished towns and villages on the Siberian tundra enough copies of Solzhenitsyn's *Gulag Archipelago* for each illiterate citizen."

"And when the new Russian reforms produced only the Oligarchs and KGB colonels running the show you frequently saw in Moscow starving veterans of World War II selling their medals to tourists."

"And when the leaders had no more idea than Brezhnev what to do with the vast population without any work or hope or ideas they eventually said *You are free.* With the new Russian reforms you can run in the race with the rest of the world: Alas they had no legs."

The anecdotes produce discontent in the auditorium. Some call out for Stanley Rosen, others for Geoffrey Hill.

Kantor says he's "invading" Oxota. Lyn maintains that Pushkin's friends insist that we are free to signify place but not describe it.

Kantor turns the pages of his lecture notes and quotes Bulgakov, who is himself a member of the audience.

And the unheard-of thing comes to pass. The tom's black fur bristles, and he gives off a soul-rending miaow. Then he gathers himself into a ball and, like a panther, springs right up onto Yeltsin's chest and thence upon his head. Growling, the tom sinks his plump paws into the thin, brushed-up hair of the President and, with a wild howl, twists the head around twice and tears it off the heavy neck.

A crocodile is a line, usually of children holding hands in twos.

Is being "out of line" as bad as being "over the top"? Yeltsin was out of line; Putin over the top.

Over the top of what, exactly?

XXIII

The black tom says, licking his paws, I only want to live in the present.

Professor Rosen also wants to live in the present but, being a philosopher, he also wants to know just what that means. Is he "out of line"? Is he "over the top"?

He finds much of what has occupied us here more "in the past" or even "in the future" than he would like. But if you're going to live in the present, you actually have to believe in "presence."

Stanley believes that human beings produce time. But here's the catch: "If human activity produces time rather than filling or occupying it like a place or structure of places that already exists, then it makes no sense to ask for the temporal location of this activity."

"If I produce time, then the activity of production must be atemporal."

It's all too much for Marie Étienne, who had that figured out already.

Also presence means to be present before.

As she is present before the hundred horses.

Stanley says "It's eros that produces time. Back to Plato, folks."

The terribly ferocious cat the size of a pig again intervenes.

He puts his paw in the air and asks for recognition.

Lyn tells him that he's come to the wrong seminar. He shouldn't be in Stanley's but in Arcadii's.

They all exist in present time, even Geoffrey Hill.

So Stanley's wrong? *The metonym*, says Lyn, *reduces the monument.*

XXIV

I myself had a large black tom called Weltschmerz. He had a sister called Zeitgeist, but this is not her story. Weltschmerz had kidney problems at a time when I was totally consumed looking after my ailing wife. The tom required care that I couldn't give, nor could I give him away to someone else because of his condition. In the end, I turned him out. I will never forget his look of astonishment and fear. He had never been outdoors before. I had told him that he would have to live in the present, and out in the wide world into which he would be flung. He hung around the house for several days howling, but finally disappeared.

We are told there are no black toms in Oxota. But I knew a black tom whose actual name was Oxota. And another called Baruch. And a third The King of a Hundred Horsemen. (In my *Directory of Black Cats*, it is true that I can find no tom called Geoffrey Hill.)

When my wife got up that morning, she asked me "Where is Weltschmertz?"

I had to tell her the truth, and so I said "Weltschmerz had to leave."

I will never forget her look of astonishment and fear.

She had hallucinations in those days.

Lyn says: "a growling crow is threatening to set fires."

If your house is burning down it is hard to live in the present.

I am present before my house.

I no longer have a black cat called Weltschmerz.

I no longer have a wife called Diana.

Lyn says: "A boy replaced his saxophone with stones."

Stanley says: *es gibt Sein* is untranslatable.

Once I was present before my black cat, Weltschmerz.

XXV

They say to those who fall ill or grieve for someone lost forever: Live for the day, live in the present, be a presence in your world.

I have no world. The only world is the world, and the world worlds as Herr Heidegger says.

Nor am I really present. Absence sounds about right.

From my friends.

From the life I used to lead.

Emptiness sounds about right.

Which is why I live in other people's books. His or hers. Theirs. The pronouns have a newly acquired bounce. Some individuals are a *They*.

"Our experience of the present is 'specious' only in the sense that it cannot be measured by public or clock time. This is because it is not a unit of temporal flow. It is rather the point of organization for all experience of temporal flow."

But "specious" sounds about right.

"Clock time" sounds about right.

I am a spider who cannot spin its web.

Line 12
Line 13
Line 14

XXVI

Or find his cat when the world that worlds takes away his wife.

Here kitty kitty kitty. Come home Weltschmerz.

Woe, World Sorrow said Father Hopkins, S.J.

You see at once it's best for me to live in someone else's book, At the present. At this time.

Also perhaps in the future. I am like a lily in the field which neither . . .

Nor

And that's not Either/Or.

Should I toil and spin? Like the spider making its present as it weaves? Or should I understand, like a resident of Oxota, that freedom is the recognition of necessity, and clean up the kitchen in my communal apartment?

Ontologies, Epistemologies, can these be achieved with Ordinary Language?

Or just articulation of despair?

Teleology respects theology, Mr Baruch, Mr. Hill. That's sure as hell.

But even Professor Rosen cannot translate *es gibt Sein.*

I am a missing cat.
I am a lily in the field.

XXVII

Ha! What utter nonsense.

But a person? It's hard to remember what such being entails.

Certainly a person is present at events in his life, though I seem often to have been absent.

How can one be absent from the events in his own life?

Eventually.

As an eventuality.

As an evacuee.

As an evader.

As an evanescing evanescent evangel, thank God.

In Evanston, Illinois.

As an evasive evasion.

As an event in the evening.

As evensong.

Evidently evincing. Something. Nothing at all. Everything at once. Evoking an evolute. In its evolution. Which exacerbates. Or is sometimes exact. You'd say I exaggerate. I claim exaltation. Take X as your example. Draw forth Excalibur. Enough of that, yes? Eh? Eh?

XXVIII

Ah, Stanley. How can somebody so wise be with us no longer. I think you were the smartest man I've ever known. That year when we both lived outside Cambridge in the village of Little Shelford I had heard your praises sung by those from King's anticipating your arrival. (King's College of A Hundred Horsemen, Marie.)

One day Diana returned from a walk and said that she must have seen you crossing the bridge because an impressive little man had his finger up in the air and was saying to a companion, "It's all in the Logos."

It turned out that she was right, and before too long we managed to get both you and Geoffrey into our kitchen for a post-Thanksgiving helping of carrot cake, Diana's British substitute for pumpkin pie.

You scoffed at Diana's carrot cake saying, "It's not like pumpkin pie at all," and told me there were only three good poems in my first book. Still, you had read the book, and you asked for seconds of the cake.

We spoke in ordinary language, just like Mr. Acker, the Shelford gardener who came along with the house. For he was with us at that table too, and when he referred to you as "his nibs," everybody laughed. As Geoffrey wrote in his poem "Discourse" which I've quoted before, you were "magisterial in your own conviction, / And a clown with it, and a judge of clowns." And you had no answer for Acker or "his nibs."

Answer, Acker, Answer: A song.

And when Geoffrey came to Notre Dame I introduced him to Joseph Buttigieg, father of our future president, who listened patiently to what he was saying — holding forth on

Jesuits — until I had to interrupt and say, "but then, you know, Joe was himself a Jesuit," and Geoffrey, feeling perhaps momentarily like a clown, muttered darkly, "Well, a great loss for the order." I've said that before.

Order, I suppose, is what I've been concerned with here. But it's mainly been an order of non sequiturs. Non sequiturs are a species of "free association," but we understand that no association is free; I've said that before. I was taken to a hearing and forced into a nuthouse because I was distraught when my wife no longer knew me. It was held against me that I had "called the ambulance three times." So I did, but twice she would not go with the first responders, so preoccupied she was with her hallucinations.

Oh, Diana. And you, Stanley, called her "Strangeways."

They took away my keys, my credit cards, my clothes, my watch, and eventually my mind.

I felt I'd been lobotomized.

I could not eat or drink or sleep.

When I refused to take the meds, they threatened ETC.

And though I do mean ETC I'm planning soon to stop.

XXIX

They said my "treatment" was "court ordered."
My companions were nine black adolescent girls.
My daughter phoned the only man she knew living in the town where I had been abducted: "My mother's dying and my father's in the psych ward there."
Where / There is the rhyme.
I was released in the care of other people's books.
Line 6
Answer, Aker, Answer.
His nibs.

Begin here the Grosse Fuge/Grande Fugue, Opus 133: I've put on the CD, Tokyo String Quartet. "Free association": I just heard that the Shinzo Abe, former Japanese P.M. has been assassinated. Non sequitur: Opus 130 has an alternate Finale [Rondo] Allegro. Free association: Gunshots in the night. Non sequitur: Diana had Parkinson's disease but died of Covid. Free association: Laura, Elliot, Ian and Leila . . . Daughter, Son-in-law, Grandson, Granddaughter.

Line 10

Random: So does an American memorize and extemporize writings.
Random: The city was suspended.

Does the city hang in the air, or is it abolished.

Line 14

XXX

There are thirty sections in Geoffrey's *Mercian Hymns*. Luckily enough they have to do with King Offa and not Baruch or Justin. And E.P.'s *A Draft of XXX Cantos*, Farrar & Rhinehart (1933), also argues for a pause.

That first Random Pick was from *Oxota*.
Happy families are all alike.
Say something, Marie.
N'empeche.
Any last words Stanley?
Nevertheless.
The Presto only lasts for a minute and fifty-seven seconds.
But the Grosse Fugue is longer than the opening Adagio.

Ten
Eleven
12

And when we lived in Little Shelford outside Cambridge our front door was very wide. Several times some ducks walked in, and one time 13 sheep.

XXX/14 must mean home.

After Echo Home / Emoh or Enough Anon Already

39 or XXXIX

LLIH and out of code: Dixit "Newton was a type of gnostic . . ."

Dixit: "And my late reasonable style appears to derive from the Gnostic Bible"

Tixid Taxi: "Grandest poetics"

"Perform their mystic dance"

"Ecnad citsym rieht mrofrep"

Eh? Eh?

"Of savagely disputed provenance"

The Players

Starring Marie Etienne, *King of a Hundred Horsemen*
Lyn Hejinian, *Oxota: A Short Russian Novel*
Geoffrey Hill, *The Book of Baruch by the Gnostic Justin*

With Mikhail Bulgakov, *The Master and Margarita*
Baruch Ben Nariah, *The Apocalypse of Baruch*
Stanley Rosen, *Metaphysics in Ordinary Language*

Quotes from the players are mostly in italics.

Afterword (or asyoulikeit)

1. Nindoddy Knows

Nindoddy knows the password
Pass-a-word
Or if a name
                    try knottingnought
or nothing doing, pal
I caught you!

Who'd like to be Ab-im-e-lech
        Abimelech is I

just as an example (rhymes
with pal) & sought
him out, or up
                              S'daisy now)
Heil Tola
Heil Dodo damn your soul

                    one kind of hi there
don't you see
I said *you had* said or should have
If your name had been Said's

brook of Judges is by jingo shallow
& bebrowed
everybody lapsing back to Baal

sat on a lap I did

well sing
me that well song and
all the while

danse it in and celebrate it: Late Style.

2. At the Well

though un-

intentionivied so I say again
although
                    you were against it,
even Baalim was approving
and Ashtaroth child of Ammon

though you *be* and seem
friendly seen with the Philistine
and Filipino
                    next you'd ask
a player for piano

          blazing Pi at rising sky-
high octane dollars
for your sense
of golden ratio

or full coherence when
the fresh water turns

to salt for wounds
bound by
Jephthah who was Harlot's boy

3. Book of Judges

(i.m. John Marshall & Edward Shiloh Matthias,
Ohio Supreme Court)

Spike of judicative nail & nothso
crazy, all for the lub of u
or typo two of them then
on a tandem
sung and danced, man, hey there, hi,
from middle of the Midian —

after Aaron's desperation
Josh's pleading, all those Bacchanals
do I mean barcaroles

                                        by whim of whom
in 6/8 or 12/8 time
and why not the bike of Leonardo
In the afterworld

At the door Jehovah's witnesses
are Dr Jekyll, Mr Hyde,
who seek
whatever you have sought and they
will find it — fore-fitted

and factious, father, grandfather

                                                  back of book is
beck of bot
I've told you that before

Other books by John Matthias
published by Dos Madres Press

Revolutions-a collaboration (2017)
with Jean Dibble & Robert Archambeau

Regrounding a Pilgrimage (2018)
with John Peck

Tales Tall & Short
fictional, factual & in between (2020)

Some Words on Those Wars (2020)

Living with a Visionary (2021)

Sight Lines (2022)
with Laura Matthias Bendoly